P9-CRB-082

JUVENILE DETENTION CENTERS

YOUR LEGAL RIGHTS

TERRY TEAGUE MEYER

ROSEN PUBLISHING

New York

Published in 2016 by The Rosen Publishing Group, Inc.
29 East 21st Street, New York, NY 10010

First Edition

Expert Reviewer: Lindsay A. Lewis, Esq.

Library of Congress Cataloging-in-Publication Data

Meyer, Terry Teague, author.
Juvenile detention centers : your legal rights/Terry Teague Meyer.
     pages cm.—(Know your rights)
Includes bibliographical references and index.
ISBN 978-1-4777-8036-7 (library bound) — ISBN 978-1-4994-3676-1 (pbk.) — ISBN 978-1-4994-3677-8 (6-pack)
1. Juvenile corrections—United States—Juvenile literature. I. Title.
KF9825.M49 2015
365'.420973—dc23

2014037934

Manufactured in the United States of America

For many of the images in this book, the people photographed are models. The depictions do not imply actual situations or events.

CONTENTS

INTRODUCTION

At sixteen years old, Kalief Browder was arrested on accusations of taking a delivery truck for a joyride and crashing it into a parked car. However, according to Browder he only watched a friend steal the truck. Overwhelmed by the juvenile justice system, Browder pled guilty because he felt that he had no defense. Despite his minor involvement in the crime, Browder was sentenced to probation and earned youthful offender status. When he was picked up on suspicion of stealing a backpack eight months later, his probationary status contributed toward the judge's decision to put Browder in detention pending a trial. It took three years for Browder to navigate the justice system and secure his freedom once again. Browder's story is an extraordinary example of the justice system gone wrong, but it serves to illustrate the importance of knowing your rights and avoiding unintended consequences of involvement in the justice system.

According to the U.S. Department of Justice (DOJ), American police and law enforcement agencies arrested 1.6 million people under the age of eighteen in 2010. This report (released in December 2013) included serious crimes such as rape and murder. The report also included arrest statistics for lesser crimes such as loitering (which involves hanging out in an area without good reason) and curfew violations (such as driving or being out in public past a certain hour). An earlier study by the University of North Carolina showed that nearly one in three young adults gets arrested by age twenty-three. Many of these arrests are for nonviolent crimes such as under-age drinking or drug possession.

Young people under the age of eighteen can be arrested for violating the rules of their school or community as well as for serious crimes. Many factors determine what happens after the arrest.

According to the DOJ, sixty-six thousand juveniles were held in different types of detention centers around the country in 2010. In one sense, these young people were lucky. They didn't end up jailed with adults in facilities that would have been less appropriate to their circumstances and potentially more dangerous. But more than a million of those juveniles who were arrested were even luckier: they avoided getting jail time entirely.

What logic explains who ends up in a juvenile detention center and who avoids jail time? This resource aims to

trace the path that can potentially lead to juvenile detention as well as the many other paths that can help young
people avoid being locked up. It is important to know how
crimes and misdeeds are defined and classified in terms of
severity, or how serious they are. Knowing your rights and
making good decisions in a tough situation can have an
impact on the rest of your life. Nobody wants to find out
about the juvenile justice system from personal experi-
ence. This resource can help you know your rights when it
comes to facing time in a juvenile detention center.

CHAPTER 1

SAY WHAT? UNDERSTANDING THE LINGO OF THE JUVENILE JUSTICE SYSTEM

Lawyers, police, and those who work with them often use special terms whose meaning may be unclear to others. Understanding this legal language is an important first step in learning how to navigate the legal system. It is also helpful in understanding the process that could lead up to detention in a juvenile facility.

Certain legal terms seem to hide their harsher meaning. For example, being in police custody essentially means that somebody has been placed under arrest.

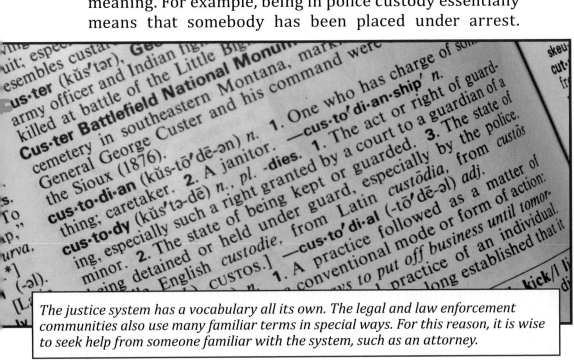

The justice system has a vocabulary all its own. The legal and law enforcement communities also use many familiar terms in special ways. For this reason, it is wise to seek help from someone familiar with the system, such as an attorney.

Similarly, being in detention means that somebody is being held in jail. In the context of juvenile detention, this implies the equivalent for juveniles of jail. In day-to-day life, to offend somebody usually just means that you have hurt his or her feelings. In the world of police and courts, an offense means breaking the law. The person who commits an offense is known as an offender.

A juvenile who ends up in court needs to be familiar with this legal lingo. For example, the document stating charges against a juvenile is called a petition and a defendant in juvenile court is called a respondent. Some terms used in the juvenile justice system differ from their equivalents in adult court. A trial in juvenile court is called an adjudication hearing. The resulting sentence or other final order is known as a disposition. However, the most important term to understand first is the word "juvenile" itself.

WHAT IS A JUVENILE?

Generally speaking, a juvenile is any young person, but the legal definition of the term can be complicated. Eighteen is the age at which citizens in the United States can vote and often begin making personal decisions without the consent of a parent or guardian. Under U.S. federal law, a juvenile is any person under the age of eighteen. If someone over the age of eighteen violates a federal law, the offense is termed a crime or a violation (depending on the severity of the offense). When a juvenile commits an offense, it is known as juvenile delinquency.

The law treats juveniles and adults differently. Why? Lawmakers have long recognized that young people are still maturing, learning, and developing—both physically and mentally. Children and teenagers are not expected to be as responsible as adults. For this reason, the law is more likely to avoid severe punishment for juveniles who make certain mistakes.

It is important to know that whether someone who violates a law is considered by the legal system to be a juvenile or an adult varies from state to state. According to the federal Office of Juvenile Justice and Delinquency Prevention (OJJDP), New York and North Carolina set the age of criminal responsibility at sixteen. Ten other states set it at seventeen and the remaining states at eighteen. This means that the same offense committed in different states could result in either juvenile or adult charges, depending on that state's laws. A juvenile delinquent is someone who breaks the law and is over the age of seven and under the age of criminal responsibility in his or her state.

Another special category exists in both federal court and New York state court that is reserved for those offenders who are on the cusp of adulthood (between the ages of sixteen and nineteen). These offenders will be tried in adult court but may be given what is known as youthful offender status. In general, juvenile or youthful offender proceedings take place in adult court, while juvenile delinquent proceedings take place in family court.

The type of offense committed is another factor that affects whether someone will be tried as an adult or a juvenile. Logically, the courts are less understanding of a young person who commits a serious crime such as murder than one who is charged with a more minor offense, such as breaking a car window or skipping school.

JUVENILES JUDGED AS ADULTS

Many young people end up in adult criminal courts despite their legal status as juveniles in their states. Juvenile cases can be waived, or transferred, to adult courts for a number of reasons. Crimes involving weapons, violence, or resulting in serious injury or death are more likely to end up in adult court. Five states allow such transfers for any criminal offense, regardless of its severity. Some states have clear guidelines defining which types of offenses can be transferred to adult court. In certain instances, legal limits known as mandatory minimum sentencing make a life sentence or other lengthy period of jail time required for certain violent crimes. This sometimes binds the courts to sentencing a juvenile who is found guilty of a crime to no less than the minimum jail time or sentence.

In 2010, the U.S. Supreme Court's ruling in *Miller v. Alabama* outlawed mandatory life in prison without parole for juveniles. Regardless of that decision, a January 2014 *New York Times* article explained that young people were still being sentenced to very long terms. For example, one fourteen-year-old was sentenced to years in prison for wounding someone during a The article also reported the story of a

Decisions by the U.S. Supreme Court influence the treatment of juveniles in the criminal justice system. The Rehnquist court (pictured here) made key decisions to protect the rights of juvenile offenders.

convicted of gun robbery and rape whose consecutive sentences totaled up to 170 years. People who are against such long sentences argue that they do not give young people a chance to learn from their mistakes.

HOW THE JUVENILE JUSTICE SYSTEM IS CHANGING

Historically, juvenile courts were quite different from adult criminal courts. Juvenile courts were less formal, and they focused on the welfare of troubled young people. However, in the 1960s, the juvenile justice system in the United States began to change. With the Supreme Court ruling in *In re Gault*, 387 U.S. 1 (1967), juvenile court defendants became entitled to many of the same protections of their rights as adult defendants. However, an important difference that remained between juvenile and adult courts was that juvenile cases continued to be tried by a judge instead of a jury. This is still true today.

The trend toward treating juvenile offenders more like adults continued in the 1970s. In the late 1980s and 1990s, the juvenile justice system and, in particular, juvenile courts became notably harsher on juveniles. Legislative changes reflected this trend. In *Stanford v. Kentucky* (1989), the Supreme Court held that sixteen- and seventeen-year-old offenders could be punished with the death penalty.

However, after the 1990s, public opinion shifted. A new trend toward greater leniency and support for troubled youth began. In *Roper v. Simmons* (2005), the Court overruled its decision in *Stanford v. Kentucky*, holding that the death penalty was a form of cruel and unusual punishment when applied to juveniles of any age. Two laws passed in 2009 marked a legislative shift mirroring the public's dwindling acceptance of a "get-tough" attitude toward juveniles. The Juvenile Crime Reduction Act aimed to reduce juvenile offenses by providing greater funding for the juvenile justice system. The Juvenile Justice Accountability and Improvement Act encouraged states to permit parole for juvenile detainees.

IDENTIFYING THE PLAYERS IN THE JUVENILE JUSTICE SYSTEM

Just as it is with the term "juvenile," the meaning of "juvenile justice system" can also vary on a state-by-state basis. The term generally encompasses all people who deal with juveniles and the law. The juvenile justice system not only handles juvenile offenders but also works for the protection and welfare of children and teens. For example, the system may be involved in removing children from neglectful or abusive parents.

Adults in many different positions deal with young people who break rules or commit offenses. School administrators who handle discipline are usually the first to deal with young offenders. Campus and municipal police are involved in initially bringing in and questioning juvenile suspects. Court administrators and social workers often play a role in assessing any family, mental health, or substance abuse problems that a juvenile may have. Their intake reports (which are the reports made when a person is arrested) help decide whether somebody should be held or released to his or her parents.

If a juvenile is charged with an offense, then he or she will deal with other important players in the justice system. Prosecutors are the attorneys who file petitions setting out charges against a juvenile. These charges formally state the offense the juvenile is accused of. Defense attorneys are the lawyers who then work to protect the rights of the accused juvenile. Probation officers are special officers who follow up after a hearing to see that

Hon. Jerome L. Fox
Circuit Court

A young person will likely deal with a number of people in the juvenile justice system, including a judge. It is important always to be respectful and cautious when dealing with participants in the juvenile justice system.

somebody who was found guilty has done what the court required after a decision was reached. All these people are involved in deciding whether or not a juvenile's offense will lead to probation, detention, or some other outcome.

CHAPTER 2

HOW DID I GET HERE? STEPS TOWARD DETENTION

What kind of offenses can lead to juvenile detention? A serious crime such as stealing a car or gravely injuring someone could land you in big trouble immediately. However, all too often a young person ends up in juvenile detention after a series of seemingly minor mistakes. A sober driver who runs a stop sign is in no immediate danger of being locked up. However if that person fails to pay the required fine or appear in court when required, then he or she is subject to larger penalties. Many juveniles become caught up in growing legal problems because they were simply unaware of the law. It is important to know the different classes of offenses and what can lead to detention in a juvenile facility. In the eyes of the law, not knowing that something is illegal is no excuse for doing it.

STATUS OFFENSES

Status offenses are actions that are only considered violations of the law when they are committed by certain people, usually minors. Examples of status offenses include curfew, truancy (failure to attend school), and alcohol violations. These laws apply only to minors, and when adults commit the actions that these laws prohibit, it is not considered illegal. Although they are not as severe as misdemeanor and felony offenses, in certain cases status offenses can lead to the detention of a juvenile. The 2011 Juveniles in Residential Placement report, published in August 2014 by the Office of Juvenile Justice and Delinquency Prevention, showed that 4 percent of juveniles in detention centers had committed status offenses.

Curfews are local rules dictating how late young people can be out at night without adult supervision. Perhaps your town has an ordinance, or rule, establishing 10 PM as a curfew during the week. That means that you could be picked up for being out with friends after that time. In some cases, curfews are used during daytime hours to discourage students from skipping school, another status offense. That means a group of teens hanging out at the mall during the school day could be picked up for and charged with curfew violations or truancy. U.S. laws that prohibit the consumption of alcoholic drinks by people under the age of twenty-one are another example of something that applies only to minors.

Other status offenses include running away from home or being incorrigible—a situation in which a parent or guardian feels his or her child's behavior is out of control and asks the courts to intervene. These kinds of offenses can be tricky. They often unintentionally involve young teenagers or children in the juvenile justice system. Parents may call the police to deal with a runaway, in hopes of

Many young people are arrested for relatively minor offenses, such as curfew violations. It is important to know the rules and regulations that are in force in your community.

simply scaring the child and forcing him or her to obey family rules. Police generally treat initial calls in these family situations as interpersonal problems and not criminal matters. However, repeated calls to the police may lead

ZERO TOLERANCE IN SCHOOLS

Many young people's problems with the law begin at school. School administrators adopt dress codes to discourage students from wearing certain clothes. A school may ban clothes that glorify drugs or alcohol, that are considered too sexy, or that might be a sign of gang membership or support. Truancy, possession of weapons or drugs, and even minor infractions of school rules can have serious consequences.

In recent years, many schools have adopted "zero tolerance" policies that leave administrators no room for leniency. Such policies are put in place to show students that administrators are serious about keeping drugs and weapons out of schools, but some schools have interpreted these rules very strictly. The punishments for even the smallest offenses have very real consequences for the students involved. Many such incidents have been reported in national media.

A February 2011 article in the Huffington Post mentions several examples of zero tolerance gone wrong. A nine-year-old was threatened with suspension for showing up at school with a toy LEGO policeman holding a gun. The article also reports that an eighth-grader in Texas was suspended for wearing rosary beads to school—something banned as a possible sign of gang involvement. Students have also gotten into serious trouble over possession of candy, mints, and cough drops, all because administrators perceived them as drugs.

Zero tolerance policies in schools make no allowances for things such as guns that are obviously toys or clothing that might, but does not, suggest gang membership.

Many question the efficiency of zero tolerance policies. A fact sheet compiled by the National Association of School Psychologists points out, "Zero tolerance policies are complex, costly, and generally ineffective." Such policies often lead to students dropping out of school. They also funnel students into the juvenile justice system—and many times into detention centers. Statistics have also shown that zero tolerance policies unfairly target minority students and students with disabilities.

In January 2014, the Obama Administration spoke out against zero tolerance policies. U.S. Attorney General Eric Holder stated, "A routine school disciplinary infraction should land a student in the principal's office, not in a police precinct." At that time, the Department of Education and the Department of Justice joined in urging schools to emphasize teaching students social skills rather than expelling or suspending them from school.

to a different result. Police who have responded to multiple calls at the same residence and have lost patience might formally detain the child and charge him or her. Many times the parents did not expect or truly desire that outcome.

FELONIES AND MISDEMEANORS: WHAT'S THE DIFFERENCE?

It makes sense for a more severe crime to bring about harsher punishment. Therefore, serious crimes—including such offenses as robbery, rape, burglary, and drug trafficking—are classified as felonies. Felonies are punishable by over a year in jail. Less serious crimes are classified as misdemeanors and are punishable by up to a year in jail. Even though they are less serious than felonies, one who is charged as an adult and convicted of a misdemeanor will have that charge on his or her permanent record, informally known as a rap sheet. Minor traffic violations such as running a stop sign constitute a third classification of

The nature of the offense and the age of the offender are important factors in determining the charges against a juvenile—and whether or not he or she will spend time in a juvenile detention center.

offense called violations or infractions. Violations are generally sealed immediately, meaning they do not remain on a person's permanent record.

In terms of detention, those who are incarcerated, or locked up, for misdemeanors are more likely to serve their sentences in a city or county jail. Terms for felonies are more often served in either a state or federal prison (depending on whether the offense committed was a state or federal crime). It is important to note, however, that not every crime leads to incarceration. In fact, misdemeanors seldom do. Fines are generally larger and other forms of punishment more severe for those committing felonies. Both misdemeanors and certain felonies can also be punishable by a term of probation rather than jail time, as well. Within their respective categories, offenses are also classified according to how serious the law considers them. Generally, a class A or class I felony or misdemeanor would be considered worse than a class C or III felony or misdemeanor. The penalties would be accordingly more severe and the risk of incarceration higher.

UNFORESEEN CONSEQUENCES

Far too often, young people find themselves in situations where a seemingly innocent or poorly thought-out action has led to unexpected consequences. A huge factor in poor decision making among teenagers is the use of alcohol or drugs. These substances can alter a person's ability to use good judgment. Teenagers are especially susceptible to acting out because of peer pressure or their emotions. What at the time may seem like an insignificant action could in fact be illegal and lead to time in a juvenile detention center.

One common example is the destruction or defacement of property. These acts legally constitute vandalism and can have serious outcomes for those who are caught. Likewise, imitation of the kinds of stunts seen on television shows and in movies can be dangerous and illegal. With the growth of social media, a far-too-common trend is not only to break the law but also make a video of the illegal activity and post it to social networks. In doing so, many young people unwittingly provide law enforcement with the evidence needed to lead to an arrest, a conviction, and sometimes a jail sentence.

SEXTING AND STATUTORY RAPE

In recent years, many young people have gotten into serious trouble for sending revealing personal photos that end up on the Internet. The problem of so-called sexting, or sending text messages and pictures of a sexual nature, has quickly gotten out of hand. Photos meant for only one recipient often end up shared with others or posted online. Once these materials are on the Internet, it can be extremely difficult to erase them or control who sees them.

In some cases, young people—even those who are legally minors in their state—who have sent, downloaded, or forwarded sexually explicit material of peers have been charged under child pornography laws. Some states do draw a distinction between teenagers who have sexted with friends that are the same age and possession of child pornography by an adult, but it is important to know that in some cases sexting can result in imprisonment and potentially a lifetime label as a sex offender.

Sexual activity between or with juveniles can lead to steep legal troubles as well. You may be familiar with the

Online pranks and so-called sexting can lead to serious legal consequences in some states. Online activity can negatively impact a young person's future in unexpected ways.

term "age of consent." The age of consent is the age at which a person is considered old enough to make the decision to consent to sexual activity. Juveniles below that age are not

considered capable of consenting. If one person is a minor and the other is not, the older person could be charged with the serious crime of statutory rape. The age of consent varies among states.

GET HIGH, GET IN TROUBLE

It is illegal for kids under the age of twenty-one to possess or drink alcohol. The use or possession of most other street drugs or unauthorized prescription drugs (including nonmedicinal marijuana) is illegal for people of any age. In 2010, about 170,600 juveniles were arrested for drug violations. Furthermore, use of these substances is a common factor among young people who engage in other illegal activities. Inexperienced teen drivers risk arrest for driving while intoxicated (DWI) or driving under the influence (DUI). Serious and even deadly accidents are a great danger. In general, teens who are drunk or high are more likely to commit vandalism, assault, or sexual assault or to disturb the peace. Possession of drugs and alcohol and the illegal activities performed under their influence can often lead to detention. In 2011, 10 percent of teens in U.S. detention centers were there for drug-related offenses.

BE CAREFUL OF THE COMPANY YOU KEEP

Law enforcement pays special attention to gang activity. It is important to be aware of any illegal activities in which your friends may be engaged. Even if you do not directly participate in illegal activity, your association with what could legally be defined as a gang or presence at the scene of a crime could implicate you, or make you appear to be guilty or closely connected to a crime in the eyes of the law.

Because gang activity is so widespread, many law enforcement agencies have special task forces devoted to fighting gangs. If suspected of gang activity, a young person taken into custody should not expect leniency. Many juveniles have received long sentences of jail time just for being at the scene of certain crimes. If you are ever in a situation where illegal activity has occurred and you were involved in any way (even if you were simply present), you should seek the advice of an attorney.

CHAPTER 3

MOVING THROUGH THE SYSTEM

While it is true that the best way to avoid detention is to avoid committing those offenses that may lead to it, once a young person is involved in the juvenile justice system, he or she should understand how the system works and what his or her rights are. Of those juveniles who are taken into custody by police, only a portion end up in long-term juvenile detention. Think of the juvenile justice system as a path with many forks. All possible routes begin with a juvenile who is suspected or accused of an offense. However, not everyone who enters the system ends up in the same place. What happens along the way and the outcome for any given juvenile depend on decisions made by a number of people, including the juvenile offender.

KNOWING YOUR RIGHTS

It is important to know your legal rights when you come into contact with somebody who is in a position of authority. These rights are named Miranda rights after the Supreme Court ruling *Miranda v. Arizona*. They assert the constitutional rights of all those suspected of committing crimes in the United States. Miranda rights help define a person's rights in encounters with police. For example, whether or not a police officer can search a car or a person without a warrant is a complicated issue. The answer varies from state to state. Generally, however, if an officer asks for your consent to search you or your car, you have the right to refuse. If the police can explain a reasonable suspicion of danger or illegal activity, they can frisk you or search the areas of your car that could be reached by you and passengers.

Most states do not give youth the right to trial by jury; a judge will hear a juvenile case. Juveniles do have, however, the Miranda right to attorneys even if they cannot afford them. It is always advisable to ask for a lawyer, even if the suspect feels the police lack evidence against him or her or that he or she is innocent. Do not waive your right to an attorney. Another Miranda right is "the right to notice of the charges against you." This means that a suspect must be told why he or she is being arrested or brought to court.

You may have heard the most famous of the Miranda rights quoted on television or in movies: "You have the right to remain silent." This is legal language that means that under the protection of the Fifth Amendment to the U.S. Constitution you do not have to answer incriminating questions during police questioning or testify if you end up in court. The decision to testify or not is the client's alone, although most people listen to their attorneys' advice when making that decision. This is unique because there are many decisions that are the lawyer's right to make (and not the client's). This is because lawyers are trained in the law and can better make those decisions. Another decision that a lawyer cannot make for the client is whether to plead guilty or go to trial.

DISPROPORTIONAL MINORITY CONTACT

One of the biggest issues with the juvenile justice system is its overrepresentation of minorities. This phenomenon is known as disproportional minority contact (DMC). Statistics show that minority youth are often more aggressively targeted for arrest and detention. While many organizations are making efforts to address the problem, minority youth offenders should be aware of this fact. If you feel you have been unfairly targeted or handled by somebody in the juvenile justice system because of your race or other minority status, tell your lawyer. He or she will help you take the right actions to best defend yourself against discrimination.

The laws and how they are interpreted vary from state to state, but constitutional rights exist nationwide. That is why it is so important to be represented by someone with legal training who can help you assert your rights. Although the process may take longer with a lawyer, the final outcome will likely be better. After all, the consequences of being in the juvenile justice system can follow you throughout your life.

FIRST BRUSH WITH TROUBLE

You are probably familiar with the administrators in charge of discipline at your school. You may also recognize the campus police who patrol school halls and parking lots. These people step in to deal with students who skip school, get into fights, or bring drugs, weapons, or other illegal objects or substances to school.

School administrators and campus security officers should be treated with respect. A young person's interactions with such individuals may make the difference between getting out of trouble and getting in deeper.

In your local community, city police officers and municipal constables or deputy sheriffs are tasked with enforcing local and state laws. They may pick up and question young people for a variety of status offenses ranging from seemingly innocuous curfew violations to more serious felonies including auto theft and arson (starting a fire).

A young person's interactions with these figures and their handling of accusations against the juvenile can greatly affect whether or not that young person quickly exits the juvenile justice system or heads farther down the path to detention. Always be courteous and cooperate, but also know and exert your constitutional rights.

THE SAME STORY WITH DIFFERENT ENDINGS

There are a number of ways to get out of the juvenile justice system without ending up in a juvenile detention facility. Some offenders may even be able to leave the system without a criminal record. Let's follow some possible routes.

Let's say Jack and Diane are caught spray painting slogans on a highway underpass. A police officer stops and talks to them but decides that they do not seem like gang members. He believes them when they say that they've never painted graffiti before, so he simply takes each of them home and speaks with their parents.

Alternatively, the police officer may not believe the teens, and he might take them to the station. He has caught them spray painting graffiti—an illegal activity. The police department may then handle this as a station adjustment, which typically means the pair will receive a warning, and a notation will be made in police files about what happened. On the other hand, the police might move Jack and Diane to an intake unit. Trained officers will then use a list of legal criteria to decide whether to release the teens to their parents or hold them for a detention hearing.

A detention hearing is the stage where it is decided whether or not Jack and Diane should be held in detention until adjudication. At this point, most teenagers are released to the custody of their parents or guardians pending

Spray painting graffiti is definitely illegal. If caught, this young man's record and behavior at the time of arrest will influence what happens next.

adjudication. This is usually the best option at this point because the legal process can take weeks or months and involve several hearings. Some teens, however, do not have the support of their parents. If parents are unsupportive or unable to care for a juvenile offender, intake workers might call someone from social services or child protective services. These social workers decide whether or not it is in the child's best interest to be returned to his or her parents. Juveniles who cannot return home end up in temporary detention centers.

Returning a teen to parents or guardians is the likely outcome for first offenses. However, local social services may step in when parents are incapable or unwilling to accept responsibility for the child.

NAUGHTY OR NICE? CHECK YOUR ATTITUDE

Throughout the juvenile justice system, the people that a juvenile encounters often have a degree of control over the juvenile's fate. Adults at each stage of the juvenile justice system help influence the next step that a youth offender will take—whether it be toward freedom or detention.

During the intake process, authorities may decide that a juvenile needs counseling or health services. For example, the Harris County Juvenile Probation Department in Houston, Texas, provides residential, health, and education services. "Residential services" refers to a screening to help decide where the juvenile will be placed. One option is at home on supervised probation. Another possibility is in a diversion program. Diversion programs are designed to keep young people out of detention facilities. Both detention facilities and diversion programs will be covered at a later point in this resource.

PUT YOUR BEST FACE FORWARD

Those who work in the juvenile justice system use written guidelines to help make decisions about juvenile offenders, but personal attitudes and opinions can influence how someone views and handles a juvenile. Such things as good grades, a stable home environment, and no previous record make it less likely for a young person to be incarcerated. A respectful, polite manner could also help. However, being courteous and listening to the authorities does not mean that you must speak with them or that you should not demand an attorney. You also have the right to ask them if you are under arrest. It is your right to ask this question and you should exercise that right if there is any question in your mind as to whether you are free to go or not.

In his book, *Overcoming the Magnetism of Street Life: Crime-Engaged Youth and the Programs that Transform Them*, former youth counselor Trevor Martin tells the story of Reggie, a first-time offender who pled guilty to robbery and was assigned to an alternative to incarceration, or ATI, program. Reggie did not complete the program and had to

A young person's clothing, manner, and speech can do a lot to impress the authorities and make them see a teenager as someone who deserves another chance.

appear before a judge for sentencing. As the judge was reviewing his past behavior, Reggie interrupted the judge using foul language. Shocked, the judge sentenced Reggie to the maximum of ten years. By completing the ATI program, Reggie could have gotten five years of probation.

Reggie's is an extreme example of foolish behavior with terrible consequences, but any youth offender should do everything possible to come across as serious and respectful, especially during a judicial hearing. Wearing appropriate clothes, such as what would be worn to church or a wedding, is key. Skirts should not be too short or necklines too low. Baggy pants and flip-flops are not appropriate. If possible, try to cover up tattoos and remove excessive piercings, too.

CHAPTER 4

WHERE WILL I END UP?

There are several reasons why the justice system uses detention centers. One is that detention facilities keep offenders off the streets, thus making society safer. Detention is also used to punish offenders and discourage them from committing future offenses. This concept is called deterrence. If there were no penalties for breaking the law, people might not take laws seriously.

Another aim of incarceration is rehabilitation. Rehabilitation is the process of preparing an offender for successful reintegration into normal society. Its goal is to teach an offender to behave in a lawful way after release. The prison system is also called the correctional system because one of its aims is to correct behavior.

There are a variety of facilities that hold young offenders. Some emphasize punishment and others stress rehabilitation. Where a youth offender ends up depends on where he or she lives, the severity of the offense, and whether or not he or she is a repeat offender.

SO MANY PLACES TO DO TIME

Juvenile detention centers come in many forms—large and small, public and private. They may be group homes in cities

After-school or all-day school detention is a common form of punishment for minor school infractions. Those who commit more serious offenses are often sent to alternative campuses.

or suburbs, or they may be ranches or camps in wilderness areas. The OJJDP's 2011 Juveniles in Residential Placement bulletin includes a census of the residents in the 2,047 juvenile

facilities operating that year in the United States. In 2011, these facilities held a total of 61,423 offenders. Just over 50 percent of these facilities were publicly operated. Publicly operated facilities held about 69 percent of juvenile offenders. While you may imagine these detention centers are like the jails you've seen on television or in movies, there are a variety of juvenile detention programs that differ greatly from each other.

OFF TO CAMP

Some juveniles are sentenced to serve time in a boot camp or wilderness program. Boot camps are residential programs that stress military-style discipline and physical conditioning. They are intended to focus more on rehabilitation than the other goals of detention. Typically, juveniles stay in boot camps for fewer than ninety days, and the programs are to be followed by a six-to-nine-month after-care program. Many boot camps and wilderness programs are privately run. Some parents voluntarily send their children, paying high prices to take serious disciplinary action.

Some short-term residential programs for delinquent teens feature military-style discipline, physical conditioning, and physical challenges.

Boot camps are less expensive than traditional incarceration, although comparable in costs to juvenile probation programs. In terms of their success, research by the OJJDP has shown that boot camps don't have a lasting effect on keeping kids out of trouble. The OJJDP's evaluations attributed the high recidivism rates among former boot-camp participants to the low funding and inefficiency of the aftercare programs. Worse yet, many believe that the measures taken by boot camps are too harsh and potentially dangerous. Some juveniles have been injured or killed in such programs. In January 2006, fourteen-year-old Martin Anderson died from suffocation in a northwest Florida boot camp after guards forced him to continue running laps despite his complaints of exhaustion.

GROUP HOMES

According to the 2011 Juveniles in Residential Placement report, group homes holding twenty or fewer residents were the most common type of juvenile detention facility. They housed 42 percent of committed juvenile offenders in 2011.

According to Patricia E. Campie, former director of the National Center for Juvenile Justice, group homes were created in the 1960s as a cheaper alternative to larger facilities. However, as with boot camps, there have been issues with group homes. Campie explains that abused or neglected youth who have been removed from their families sometimes must live with those who are serving criminal sentences. Research has shown that the influence of juvenile offenders on other youth in the facilities contributes to overall greater juvenile delinquency. Furthermore, group homes do not always offer the health services and support available to residents in larger institutions.

IT'S HARD TO ESCAPE

Juveniles who are adjudicated for serious offenses are more likely to end up in secure detention centers. In 2011, 11 percent of committed juvenile offenders were held in detention centers. Secure detention centers are more

ALL ALONE

A major problem in juvenile detention facilities is the use of solitary confinement. Many juveniles are locked up without contact with others for hours a day for periods lasting days or sometimes months. Solitary confinement is often used as a punishment for causing trouble or failing to follow rules.In other cases, LGBTQ (lesbian, gay, bisexual, transgender, and queer or questioning) youth offenders are isolated, often for their own protection.

In January 2014, New York State agreed to make changes in its policy of disciplining juveniles by putting them in solitary confinement. Under this agreement, sixteen- and seventeen-year-olds would be allowed at least five hours a day of programs outside their cells. Previously, the New York City Board of Corrections had reported that three mentally ill teens were each serving two hundred days in solitary, confined for twenty-three hours a day.

The American Civil Liberties Union (ACLU) is working to change such situations. In August 2013, the organization issued a Solitary Confinement Scorecard. The ACLU noted that Texas, Nevada, Florida, and Massachusetts were changing policies on solitary confinement. Nonetheless, many states are slow to introduce these reforms, and in some cases, the modified policies still permit deplorable conditions.

similar to adult prisons than other forms of juvenile detention. Not all long-term juvenile detention centers are alike, but conditions are generally unfavorable. Reports by juvenile justice advocates who seek changes within the system paint a dismal picture of life inside detention centers.

According to a 2010 report by the OJJDP, larger facilities (those with more than two hundred residents) were more likely to lock youth up during sleeping hours. Many used intense security measures such as locked gates and fences or walls with razor wire on top. One in four facilities reported using such restraints as handcuffs, leg cuffs, and leather straps to deal with out of control residents. Locking up youth in seclusion for four or more hours was another reported means of controlling unruly residents.

WILL I BE SAFE?

Sadly, your safety is not guaranteed in a detention center. Reports nationwide tell of juveniles physically or sexually assaulted by guards or other inmates while they are in detention. U.S. Congress passed the Prison Rape Elimination Act (PREA) of 2003 to begin to deal with the problem. One requirement of this law is to survey reported sexual abuse in juvenile facilities. According to the Bureau of Justice statistics, the report surveyed 326 juvenile facilities representing all fifty states. During a period of twelve months, 9.5 percent of those surveyed experienced one or more incidents of sexual victimization, either by other juvenile residents (2.5 percent) or by staff members (7.7 percent). In some cases, they were coerced with the offer of favors, protection, alcohol, or drugs in exchange for sex.

The number of incidents reported varied across facilities and states. Georgia, Illinois, Ohio, and South Carolina reported the highest rates of victimization of all states. Delaware, Massachusetts, New York, and the District of Columbia reported no sexual victimization—a fact that

PROBLEMS MADE WORSE BY INCARCERATION

Studies have shown that youth with gender-identification issues and female teenagers face greater difficulties while being held in juvenile detention centers. Furthermore, juveniles with mental health issues or drug addictions often don't receive the treatment they need. These young people may sometimes be isolated for their own protection, but this isolation also punishes them.

According to the *New York Times*, a one-day survey carried out in July 2013 in New York City found "102 of the 140 teenagers in solitary were either seriously or moderately mentally ill." Lack of funding for enough properly trained staff is a recurring problem. Limited budgets and the need for funds in other sectors often lead voters and legislators not to prioritize the treatment of juvenile delinquents.

In 2013, the State of New Jersey's Juvenile Justice Commission paid a four-hundred-thousand-dollar $400,000 settlement in response to a lawsuit brought by the Juvenile Justice Center on behalf of two boys who had suffered long periods of solitary confinement in state juvenile detention facilities. Neither of the boys received mental health treatment during their extended periods in solitary confinement. Solitary confinement also made their mental problems worse. According to Sandra Simkins, one of the attorneys who represented the case, the facility responded to requests for help or complaints about conditions by extending their periods of solitary confinement. Many facilities use names such as "prehearing room restriction," "segregation," or "close watch" instead of "solitary confinement." Such names seek to disguise the harsh conditions of the practice.

many advocates do not accept at face value. It is important to know that real rates of victimization in detention facilities do not necessarily correspond to the statistics that those facilities report. LGBTQ youth are more likely to be victimized than other juvenile offenders in detention.

WHAT WILL I LEARN?

The OJJDP reports that most juvenile detention centers (92 percent) have some sort of educational program. Typically, a student's school records are evaluated soon after arrival. Educational opportunities vary depending on the size and type of facility. However, taken as a whole, 91 percent of facilities offer high school education and 84 percent offer middle school instruction. Many facilities have special education services (82 percent) and preparation for GED (general equivalency diploma) testing (71 percent). Only 38 percent offer technical education, and 31 percent offer postsecondary education (the equivalent of college programs).

Juvenile offenders should not expect in-detention education to be the same quality as that of regular public schools. The Children's Defense Fund (CDF) considers improving education for youth in detention an important priority. The CDF reports that "only 45 percent of youth in the juvenile justice system spend at least six hours a day in school."

HEALTH CONSIDERATIONS

According to the OJJDP, juveniles are routinely assessed for mental health issues soon after entering a facility, most often

The American Civil Liberties Union (ACLU) is one of several organizations working to protect individual rights and improve conditions for juveniles and adults in the criminal justice system.

by in-house mental health professionals. Many facilities provide counseling or treatment for residents with substance abuse problems. Detention centers may also provide individual counseling and group therapy.

As with sexual assault rates, official reports may not always accurately reflect reality. Such organizations as the ACLU and the Juvenile Justice Center have issued reports claiming that many juveniles in detention do not get the help they need. Counseling or treatment may be inadequate or sessions may be too infrequent.

CHAPTER 5

ALTERNATIVES TO DETENTION

Serving time in a secure detention facility is difficult. The fastest way out is to keep a low profile and follow the rules. Causing trouble while in detention can lead to a longer sentence. If you feel that you are being treated unfairly in a detention center, work through trusted adults such as your lawyer, counselor, or staff at the facility that you trust to try to change the situation. A number of groups exist to help young people in trouble with the law. These groups are working to improve conditions for juveniles in detention.

WHAT IS RECIDIVISM?

Many people who serve time in detention after an offense change their behavior and keep out of trouble after being released. However, many others return to the old behaviors that involved them in the justice system in the first place. The latter is called recidivism. For example, an offender previously detained for selling drugs may go back to life as a drug dealer after being released from a detention facility. This may be because he or she feels that employment options are limited or because of pressure from old friends.

Recidivism is a serious problem for juvenile law enforcement. One of the goals of detention and probation is to teach people a lesson and prepare them to lead better lives. However, an estimated 30 to 90 percent of juveniles reoffend. Nationwide, the recidivism rate remains high even as the juvenile crime rate itself has dropped. Some people consider juvenile detention centers to be a way station leading to adult prison.

ALTERNATIVE SENTENCES

The American "get-tough" attitude toward juvenile offenders is changing. Reports of abuse, neglect, and mistreatment in juvenile detention facilities have focused attention on delinquents as victims. Lawmakers are rethinking their approach to delinquency. Inadequate funding is one major reason such institutions fail to successfully rehabilitate their charges. Juvenile detention centers are costly with disappointing results.

Keeping juveniles out of detention centers may be the best way to reform their behavior. Juvenile diversion means directing young offenders out of the juvenile justice system before the adjudication stage. This helps young people stay at home and continue schooling while subject to regular but limited supervision by a probation officer.

Judges in the adjudication process have a number of possible ways to sentence juveniles. It is less likely that a first-time offender will be sent to a detention facility for a minor crime. There are several sentencing alternatives available.

PROBATION AND PUBLIC SERVICE

Probation is a program that does not hold offenders in detention but also does not leave them totally free. Probation comes with conditions and a probation officer who makes sure that those conditions are met. One of the conditions may be restitution—paying the victim of an offense for loss or damages related to the offense. Probation often comes with the requirement of doing public service for a designated number of hours. Examples of probation

Juveniles sentenced to probation must meet regularly with an assigned probation officer who monitors the young person's progress and makes sure conditions required by the court are met.

requirements include cleaning up graffiti or picking up trash in a public park. Other probation requirements may be designed to benefit a troubled youth, such as regular meetings with a trained counselor or enrollment in a treatment program for drug or alcohol addiction.

Completion of the terms of probation is important. It could be the way to put a mistake in the past without a criminal record. Failure to obey the terms of probation will put a juvenile offender back in front of a judge or in a detention facility.

OTHER ALTERNATIVES TO DETENTION

In addition to other alternatives to detention, forty states have put other reforms in place under the Juvenile Detention Alternatives Initiative. This program began in 2006 and stresses alternative sentences for juveniles, including house arrest, day treatment facilities, and education and mentoring programs. The initiative also helps youth offenders navigate the court system, sending them reminders about appearances and even providing transportation to court.

In many states, law enforcement agencies use GPS monitoring to keep track of juvenile offenders. House arrest with GPS monitoring costs less than detention and minimizes contact between young people who are not dangerous with those in detention facilities who potentially are.

One program in Reading, Pennsylvania, allows community members to help decide the fate of young offenders. Juveniles involved in minor crimes appear with report cards before a panel of adult volunteers. The

RESTORATIVE JUSTICE: OFFENDERS AND VICTIMS MEET FACE TO FACE

The justice system in the United States has traditionally focused on the offender. Criminal penalties are designed to punish wrongdoers and act as a deterrent. Some forms of punishment also include programs that educate and rehabilitate offenders. But what about the victims? Even if the victim of a robbery recovers his or her property, that person is often left feeling insecure and violated. When a fight results in a disabling condition or a drunk driver kills somebody, there is no way to make up for that loss. Restorative justice aims to bring offenders, victims, and other interested parties together to help all parties heal. The process has been shown to benefit both the wronged and the wrongdoers.

Modern restorative justice emerged in the 1970s with experiments that brought people who committed offenses face-to-face with their victims. The idea, however, was not new. The Maori people of New Zealand, indigenous Hawaiians, and certain African cultures have used restorative justice for a long time. An example of restorative justice cited in a February 2010 article in *Minnesota Lawyer* shows how a meeting between young vandals and their victims led to a positive outcome for all. A group of teenagers had smashed a number of mailboxes. The restorative justice process brought the offenders, their parents, and the victims together to discuss the situation. In this case, the teens wrote letters of apology and made restitution, meaning they paid for the damage. Victims reported feeling better after talking about what happened and how it made them feel.

Restorative justice has shown results in Minnesota. Records show that juveniles who underwent this process were less likely to reoffend than those who received probation.

juveniles are typically sentenced to community service related to their individual talents. They also take classes on personal responsibility and write apology letters and essays. Those arrested for drug or alcohol offenses attend substance abuse programs. After completing the panel's requirements, the offenders sign contracts promising not to repeat their behavior. According to the local newspaper, the *Reading Eagle*, the program is "successful 90 percent of the time."

A sentence of hours to be spent in community service is a common alternative to detention. Such sentences benefit the community and may help young offenders learn responsibility.

Many organizations are working to reform the juvenile justice system. These reforms promote alternatives to incarceration and revised standards and training for the adults who work with juvenile offenders. Past patterns of harsh treatment seem to be shifting in a trend toward helping young people learn from their mistakes. Still, the conditions in many juvenile detention centers are little better than adult prisons. Changing laws and policies concerning juvenile offenders takes time, and much of the public still thinks that such teenagers deserve whatever punishment the system gives them. The harsh realities of juvenile detention centers are an important consideration for young potential offenders. If you are ever facing detention in a juvenile facility, the best way out is to know your rights, work with a lawyer, and be knowledgeable about the alternatives to juvenile detention.

GLOSSARY

adjudication The term used for a trial in which the accused party is a juvenile.

custody The state of being arrested or held by authorities in the criminal justice system.

deterrent Something that is meant to discourage or prevent people from committing a certain act.

disposition The final arrangement or settlement that explains the outcome of a juvenile case in family court.

diversion program Any pretrial program that serves as an alternative to incarceration.

felony A serious crime that can earn a minimum sentence of at least one year in a detention center.

incarceration The state of being held in a jail, prison, or other type of detention center.

incorrigible Demonstrating repeated or habitual defiance of the lawful orders given by a legal guardian or custodian.

juvenile delinquent A young person under the age of criminal responsibility who has committed some kind of offense.

misdemeanor A minor crime that is punishable by up to one year in a detention center.

ordinance A law or regulation established by a municipal authority.

parole Early release of an offender from a period of detention, generally as a reward for good behavior.

petition A formal criminal complaint that sets out the charges against an offender.

probation An alternative to incarceration during which time an offender is monitored and must follow a set of conditions imposed by the court and a special officer who serves as that individual's probation officer.

recidivism The tendency to return to a previous pattern of behavior, especially criminal behavior.

respondent The term for a defendant or accused party in a juvenile case.

restitution Payment or services given to the victim of an offense to make up for losses related to that offense.

status offense An action that is only considered a violation of the law when committed by a certain population, generally minors.

vandalism The deliberate destruction of public or private property.

waive To voluntarily give up a right or privilege.

American Civil Liberties Union (ACLU)
125 Broad Street, 18th Floor
New York, NY 10004
(212) 549-2500
Website: https://www.aclu.org
The ACLU is a nonprofit organization that works through U.S. courts and legislators to preserve individual rights and freedoms.

Annie E. Casey Foundation
701 St. Paul Street
Baltimore, MD 21202
(410) 547-6600
Website: http://www.aecf.org
The Annie E. Casey Foundation is a private charitable foundation working to improve living conditions for disadvantaged children and youth. One of its missions is to advance justice for juveniles.

Canadian Bar Association (CBA)
865 Carling Avenue, #500
Ottawa, ON K1S 5S8
Canada
(800) 267-8860
Website: http://www.cba.org
The CBA is a professional association that serves the legal community in Canada with development and support. The association has established a Children's Law Committee to focus on legal issues relating to youth.

Canadian Institute for the Administration of Justice (CIAJ)
Faculty of Law, University of Montreal
Pavilion Maximilien-Caron
3101 Chemin de la Tour, Room A-3421
P.O. Box 6128, Station Centre Ville
Montreal, QC H3C 3J7
Canada
(514) 343-6157
Website: https://www.ciaj-icaj.ca
The CIAJ is a nonprofit organization focused on improving the quality of justice for all Canadians. Among its projects is a conference on young people with mental health issues in the juvenile justice system.

Juvenile Law Center (JLC)
1315 Walnut Street, 4th Floor
Philadelphia, PA 19107
(215) 625-0551
Website: http://www.jlc.org
The JLC is a nonprofit, public-interest law firm whose goal is to protect the rights of children in the courts and through legislatures.

National Council on Crime and Delinquency (NCCD)
160l R Street NW, 2nd Floor
Washington, DC 20009
(800) 306-6223
Website: http://www.nccd.org
The NCCD is a nonprofit organization that applies research in criminal and juvenile justice to public policy and practice.

Office of Juvenile Justice and Delinquency
    Prevention (OJJDP)
810 Seventh Street NW
Washington, DC 20531
(202) 307-5911
Website: http://www.ojjdp.gov
The OJJDP is the office of the U.S. Department of Justice
    that supports programs dealing with juvenile delin-
    quency through research, training, and the
    development of guidelines.

WEBSITES

Because of the changing nature of Internet links, Rosen
Publishing has developed an online list of websites related
to the subject of this book. This site is updated regularly.
Please use this link to access the list:

http://www.rosenlinks.com/KYR/Deten

FOR FURTHER READING

Brezina, Corona. *Frequently Asked Questions About Juvenile Detention*. New York, NY: Rosen Publishing, 2012.

Byers, Ann. *Frequently Asked Questions About Gangs and Urban Violence*. New York, NY: Rosen Publishing, 2011.

Chura, David. *I Don't Wish Nobody to Have a Life Like Mine: Tales of Kids in Adult Lockup*. Boston, MA: Beacon Press, 2010.

Echols, Damien. *Life After Death*. New York, NY: Penguin Group, 2012.

Engdahl, Sylvia, ed. *Prisons*. Farmington Hills, MI: Cengage Learning, 2010.

Espejo, Roman, ed. *Are Teen Curfews Effective?* Farmington Hills, MI: Cengage Learning, 2009.

Gerdes, Louise, ed. *Juvenile Crime*. Farmington Hills, MI: Greenhaven Press, 2012.

Gitlin, Marty. *Understanding Your Right to Due Process*. New York, NY: Rosen Publishing, 2014.

Grosshandler, Janet, and Valerie Mendralla. *Drinking and Driving. Now What?* New York, NY: Rosen Publishing, 2012.

Lily, Henrietta M., Matthew Monteverde, and Marilyn E. Smith. *School Violence and Conflict Resolution*. New York, NY: Rosen Publishing, 2013.

Marcovitz, Hal. *Should Juveniles Be Tried as Adults?* San Diego, CA: Reference Point Press, 2012.

Merino, Noel, ed. *Criminal Justice*. Farmington Hills, MI: Greenhaven Press, 2013.

Mooney, Carla. *Teen Violence*. San Diego, CA: ReferencePoint Press, 2013.

Thompson, Stephen P., ed. *Teens at Risk*. Farmington Hills, MI: Greenhaven Press, 2013.

BIBLIOGRAPHY

Beck, Allen, et al. "Sexual Victimization in Juvenile Facilities Reported by Youth, 2012." Bureau of Justice Statistics. Retrieved March 8, 2014 (http://www.bjs.gov/index.cfm?tt=pbdetail&iid=4656).

Bergman, Paul, and Sara J. Berman. *The Criminal Law Handbook: Know Your Rights, Survive the System*. 13th Edition. Berkeley, CA: Nolo, 2013.

Bernard, Thomas J., and Megan C. Kurlychek. *The Cycle of Juvenile Justice*. New York, NY: Oxford University Press, 2010.

Chambliss, William J., ed. *Juvenile Crime and Justice*. Thousand Oaks, CA: SAGE Publications, 2011.

Edmondson-Penny, Rashida. "Why It's Important to Know Your Rights. A Guide to Young People's Rights in Juvenile Delinquency Court." National Juvenile Defender Center. Retrieved December 15, 2013 (http://www.njdc.info/gaultat40/pdfs/kyr_booklet.pdf).

Griffin, Patrick, et al. "Trying Juveniles as Adults: An Analysis of State Transfer Laws and Reporting." Office of Juvenile Justice and Delinquency Prevention, U.S. Department of Justice, September 2011. Retrieved February 28, 2014 (https://www.ncjrs.gov/pdffiles1/ojjdp/232434.pdf).

Hockenberry, Sarah. "Juveniles in Residential Placement, 2011." Office of Juvenile Justice and Delinquency Prevention, August 2014. Retrieved October 27, 2014 (http://www.ojjdp.gov/pubs/246826.pdf).

Hudson, David L. *Juvenile Justice*. New York, NY: Infobase Publishing, 2010.

National Association of School Psychologists. "Zero Tolerance and Alternative Strategies: A Fact Sheet for Educators and Policymakers." Retrieved March 3, 2014 (http://www.nasponline.org/resources/factsheets/zt_fs.aspx).

Milton, Trevor B. *Overcoming the Magnetism of Street Life: Crime-Engaged Youth and the Programs that Transform Them.* Lanham, MD: Lexington Books, 2011.

Murphy, Bridget. "In These Duval Youth, He Sees Himself. For Them, This Mentor Wants More." *Florida Times-Union*, March 1, 2010. Retrieved March 20, 2014 (http://jacksonville.com/news/metro/2010-03-01/story/in_these_duval_youth_he_sees_himself_for_them_this_mentor_wants_more).

Puzzanchera, Charles. "Juvenile Arrests 2010." Office of Juvenile Justice and Delinquency Prevention, December 2013. Retrieved January 8, 2014 (http://www.ncjj.org/pdf/242770.pdf).

Rosenheim, Margaret K. et al. *A Century of Juvenile Justice.* Chicago, IL: The University of Chicago Press, 2002.

Simkins, Sandra. *When Kids Get Arrested: What Every Adult Should Know.* New Brunswick, NJ: Rutgers University Press, 2009.

Thornton, Patrick. "Minnesota's Juvenile Justice Reform Initiatives Working, Spreading." *Minnesota Lawyer*, February 22, 2010. Retrieved November 26, 2013 (http://minnlawyer.com/2010/02/22/juvenile-justice-reform-initiatives-working-spreading).

Van Wormer, Katherine S., and Loreen Walker, ed. *Restorative Justice Today.* Thousand Oaks, CA: SAGE Publications, 2013.

Whitehead, John. "Zero Tolerance Schools Discipline Without Wiggle Room." *Huffington Post*, February 8, 2011. Retrieved March 3, 2014 (http://www.huffingtonpost.com/john-w-whitehead/zero-tolerance-policies-schools_b_819594.html).

INDEX

ABOUT THE AUTHOR

Writer and educator Terry Teague Meyer lives in the Houston, Texas, area. She has taught at the middle school, high school, and college levels. She volunteers as a youth mentor and English as a second language tutor. She has written several books for young adults. Many of her books deal with teens adapting to new and difficult situations and planning for the future.

ABOUT THE EXPERT REVIEWER

Lindsay A. Lewis, Esq., is a practicing criminal defense attorney in New York City, where she handles a wide range of matters, from those discussed in this series to high-profile federal criminal cases. She believes that each and every defendant deserves a vigorous and informed defense. Lewis is a graduate of the Benjamin N. Cardozo School of Law and Vassar College.

PHOTO CREDITS